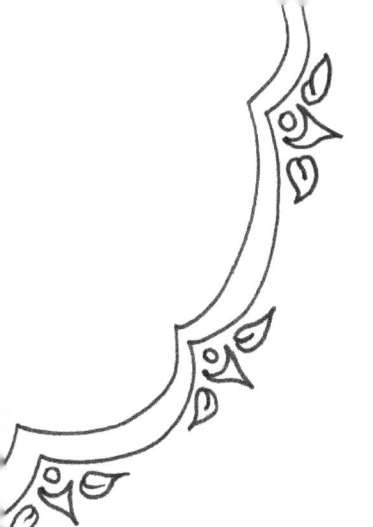

Washington D.C.

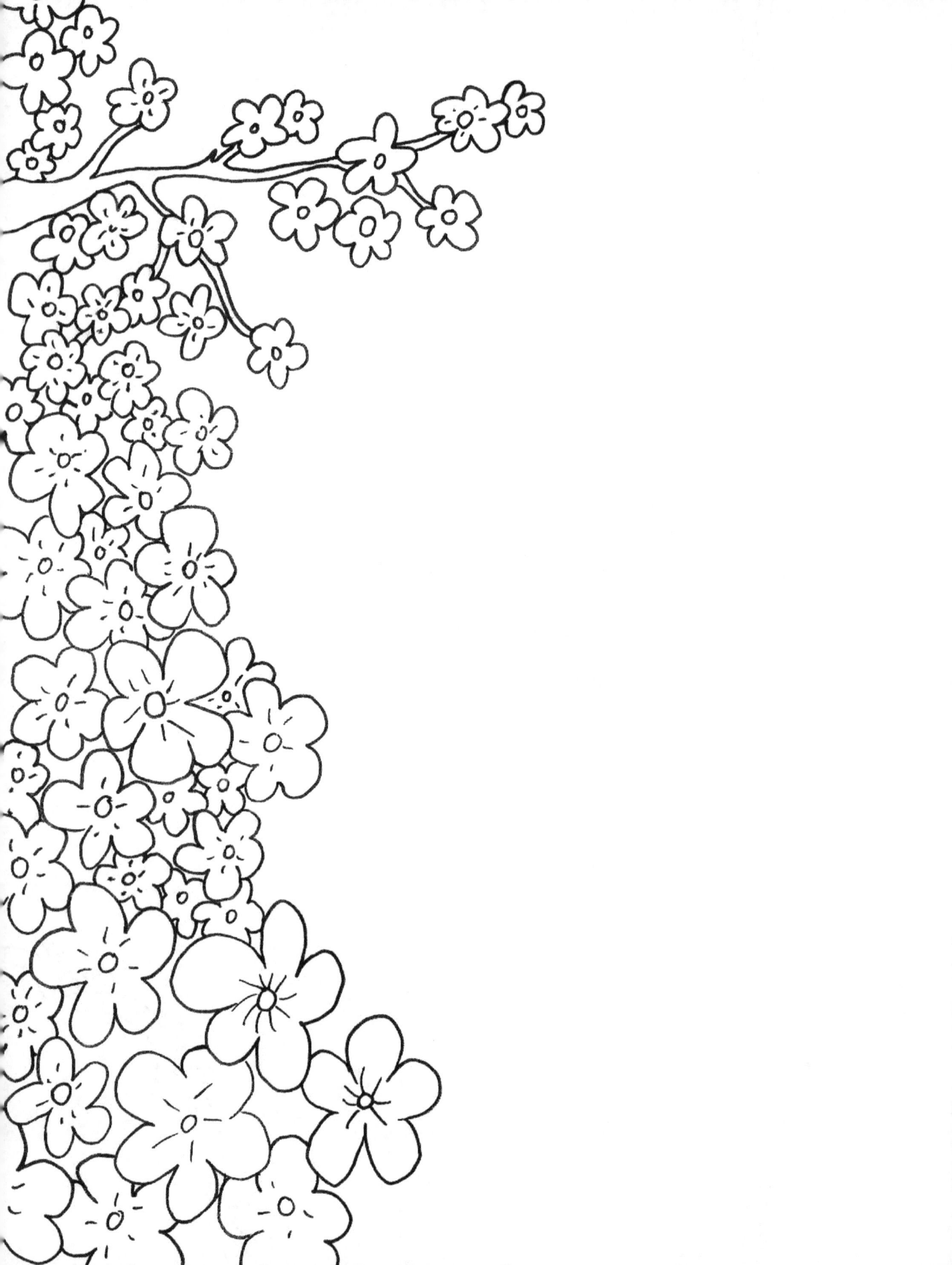

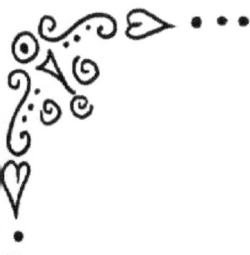

To my creative, colorful and
color-loving daughter Zena

(The lines are just suggestions)

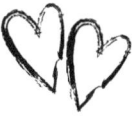

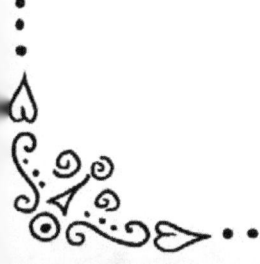

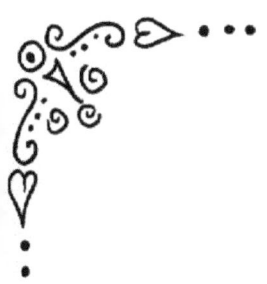
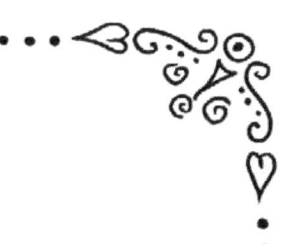

Enjoy coloring hand-drawn illustrations of:

- ☆ The White House
- ☆ Jefferson Memorial
- ☆ Smithsonian Castle
- ☆ American Flag
- ☆ Washington Memorial
- ☆ Historic Rowhouses
- ☆ Key Bridge

The White house

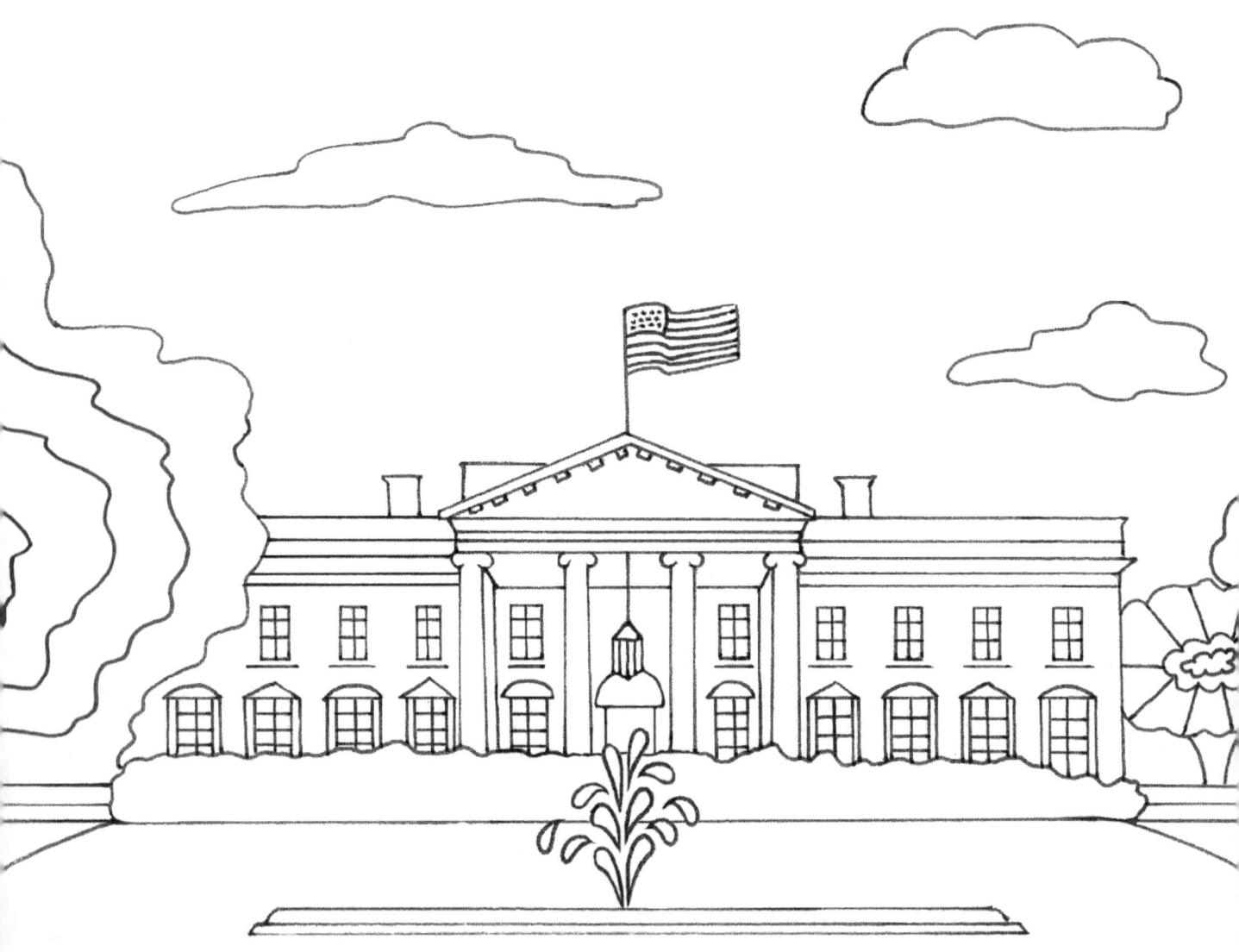

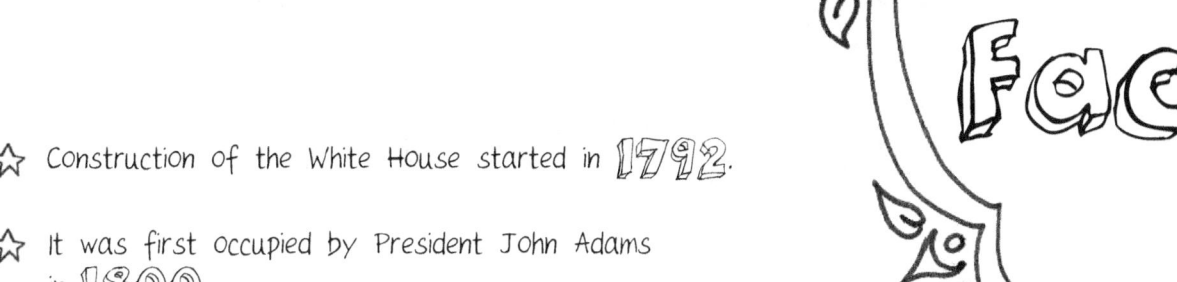

☆ Construction of the White House started in 1792.

☆ It was first occupied by President John Adams in 1800.

☆ The total cost to build it was $232,372.

☆ The building was first made white with lime-based whitewash in 1798.

☆ The White House requires 570 gallons of paint to cover its surface.

☆ There are 132 rooms, 32 bathrooms, and 6 levels.

☆ President Theodore Roosevelt officially gave the White House its current name in 1901, although it had been used as a nickname before that date.

☆ Running water was piped into the White House in 1833, running hot water in 1853.

☆ Gas lighting was installed in 1848, replacing candles and oil lamps.

☆ Central heating was installed in 1837.

☆ The White House has a tennis court, swimming pool, putting green, movie theatre, billiards table, ping pong table, jogging track and bowling alley.

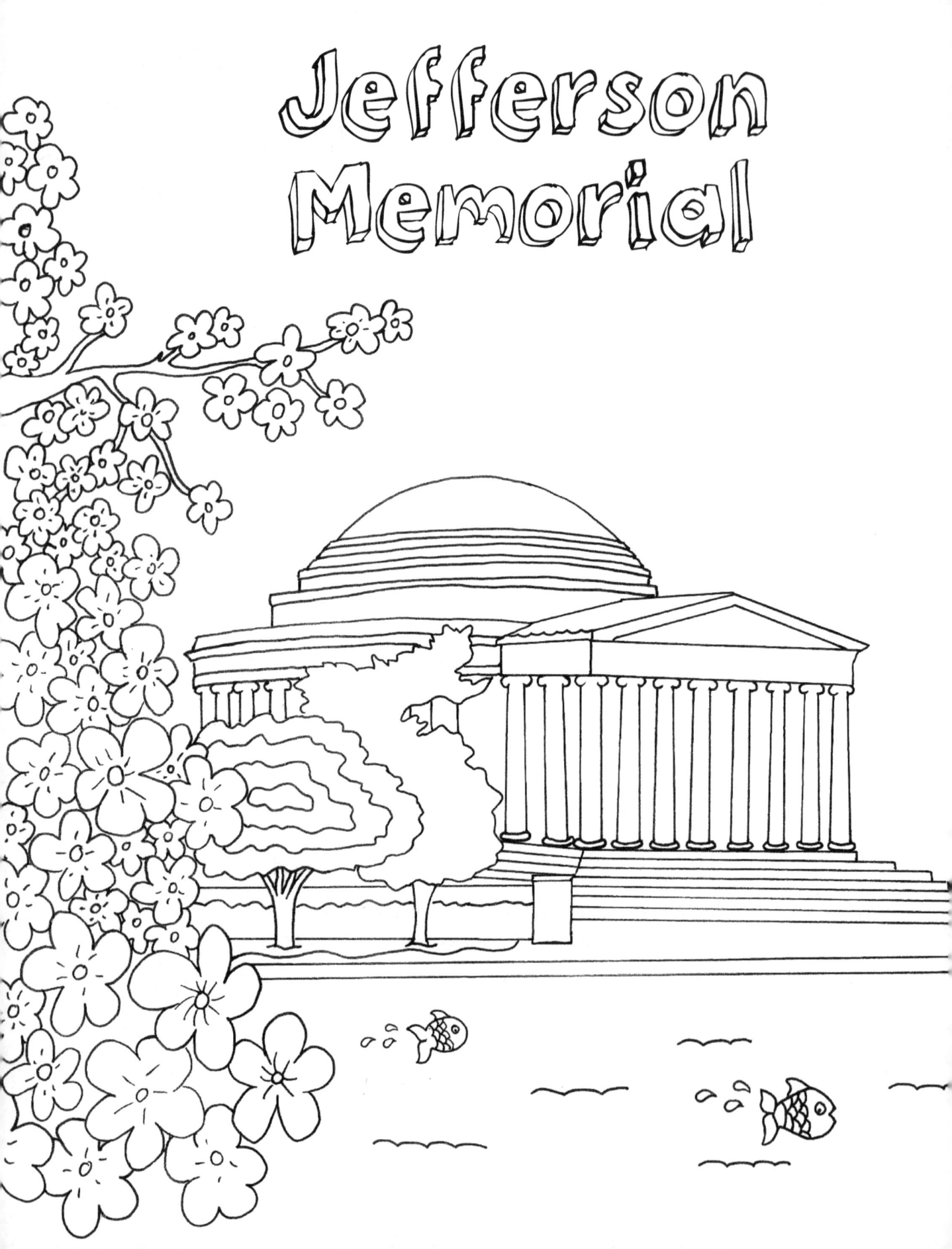

Jefferson Memorial

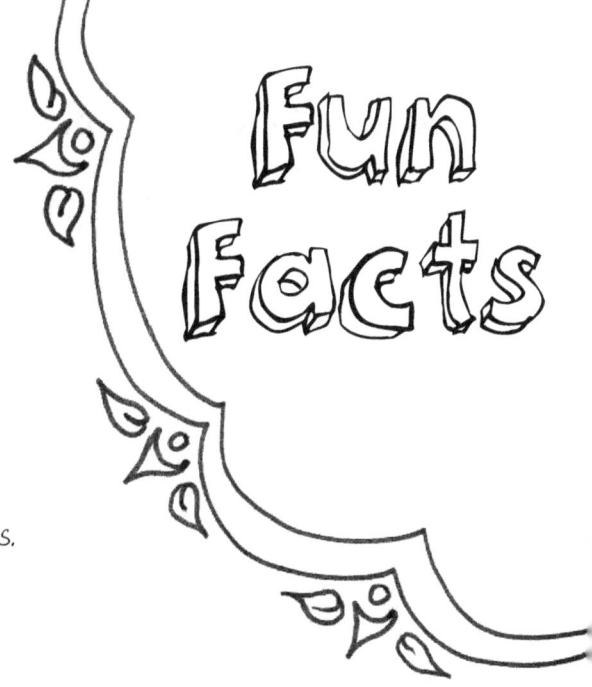

☆ The Jefferson Memorial was designed by John Russel Pope in a Classical Revival style.

☆ It is 129 ft. high.

☆ Rudolph Evans sculpted the Jefferson Statue.

☆ The statue is 19ft high and weighs 10,000 pounds.

☆ Quotes depicting letters, famous sayings and beliefs of Thomas Jefferson, and lines from the Declaration of Independence can be found on the southwest panel of the monument.

☆ The steps leading up to the building are made of pure marble.

☆ Construction began on November 15, 1939 and was completed on April 13, 1943.

Cherry Blossoms

☆ The cherry blossoms surrounding the tidal basin (and others around the D.C. area) were a gift from the people of Japan. 3,020 trees were donated in total.

☆ In Japan the flowers represent the fragility and beauty of life.

☆ In 1912 First Lady Helen Herron Taft and Viscountess Chinda, wife of the Japanese Ambassador, planted two Yoshino cherry trees on the northern bank of the Tidal Basin. Although a small ceremony, it was the inception of The Cherry Blossom Festival that continues today.

☆ The cherry blossom trees were planted around the tidal basin from 1913–1920.

☆ In 1952 the National Park Service shipped budwood from the trees to Japan to help restore the cherry tree grove along the Arakawa River in Tokyo. The grove, which provided the parent stock for Washington D.C.'s first trees, had fallen into decline.

Smithsonian Castle

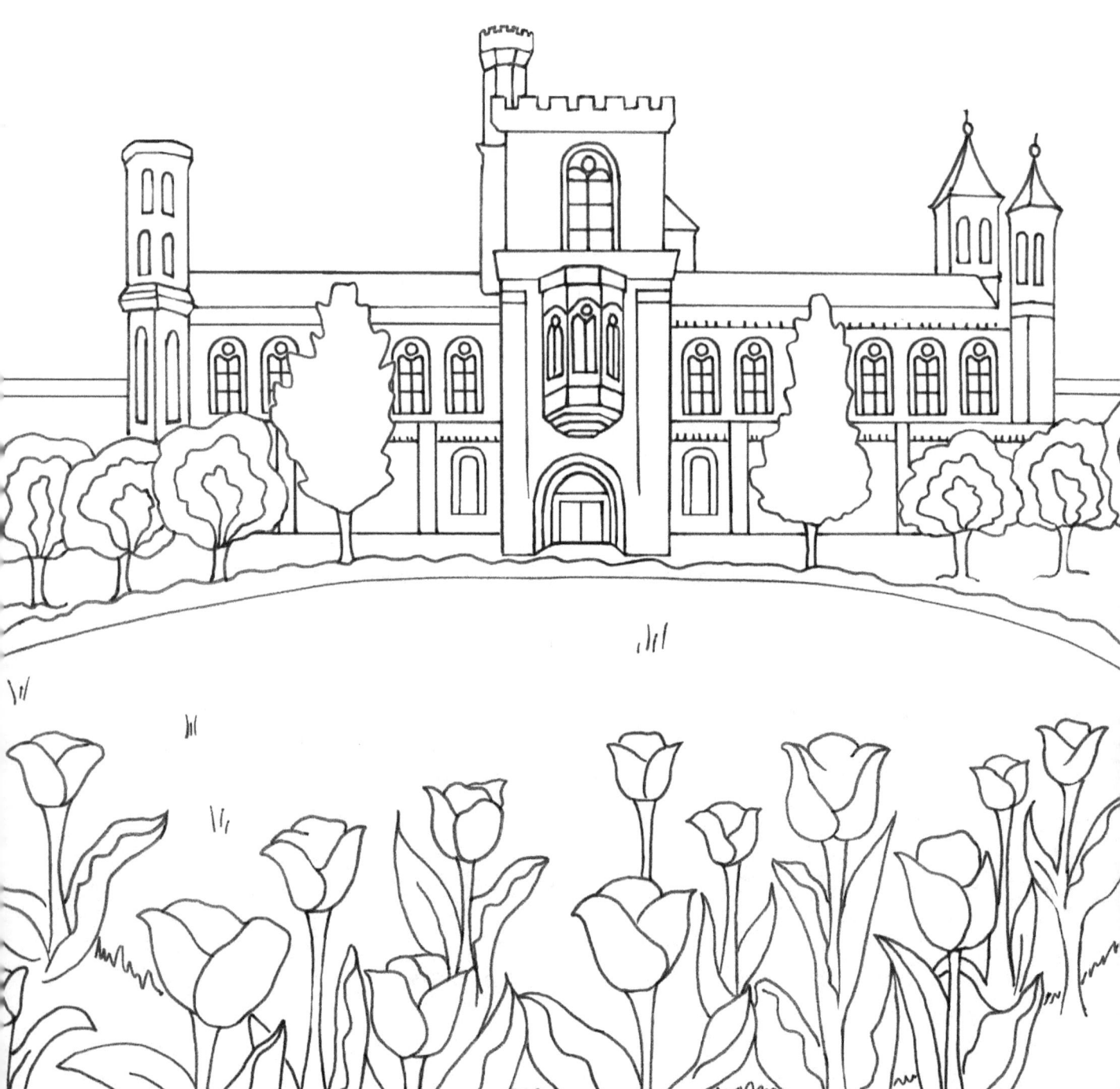

Fun Facts

☆ The Smithsonian Castle is officially known as "The Smithsonian Institution Building."

☆ It was designed by architect James Renwick, Jr.

☆ It is constructed of red sandstone from Seneca Creek in Maryland.

☆ It is designed in a Norman style of architecture, with design elements from late 12th century Romanesque and early Gothic styles.

☆ It was completed in 1855. At that time it was on an isolated piece of land, separated from downtown Washington D.C. by a canal.

☆ Major reconstruction was completed on the Castle in 1865 after a fire destroyed the upper story of the main building, and the north and south towers.

☆ It was renovated from 1968-1970 to install a modern electrical system, elevators, heating and air conditioning.

☆ In 1977 it was awarded Historic Landmark status.

☆ Over the years it has had many uses. It has been living quarters for the secretary of the Smithsonian, research and administrative offices, lecture halls, exhibit halls, library and reading rooms, chemical labs and storage areas for specimens.

☆ Today it houses the institution's administration offices and information center.

☆ ☆ ☆ ☆ ☆ ☆ ☆ ☆ ☆ ☆ ☆ ☆ ☆ ☆

American Flag

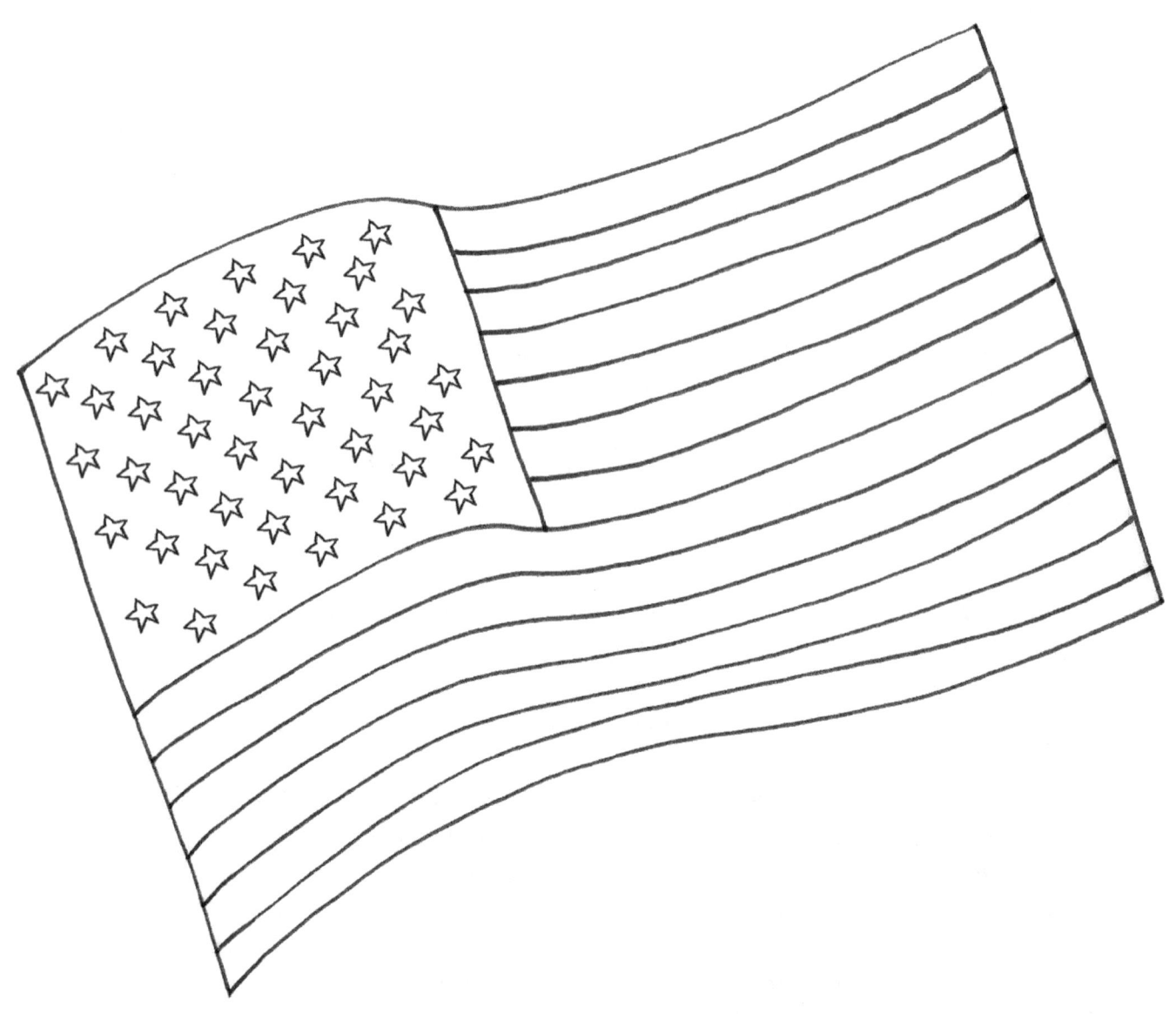

☆ ☆ ☆ ☆ ☆ ☆ ☆ ☆ ☆ ☆ ☆ ☆ ☆ ☆

Fun Facts

American flag colors:

Red: valor and bravery

White: purity and innocence

Blue: Vigilance, perseverance and justice.

☆ On June 14, 1777, Congress passed the Flag Resolution which stated that the flag would be made up of 13 strips, alternating red and white, and 13 white stars on a blue background.

☆ Flag Day is observed on June 14 every year.

☆ Stars are added when new states join the union. They are added on July 4th following the entry of the new state. There are currently 50 stars.

☆ Betsy Ross made the first flag. She was commissioned personally by George Washington.

☆ Also known as "Old Glory."

☆ Proper display of the flag is usually from sunrise to sunset, and only in good weather.

☆ If one or more flags are flown on the same pole, the American Flag must be on top.

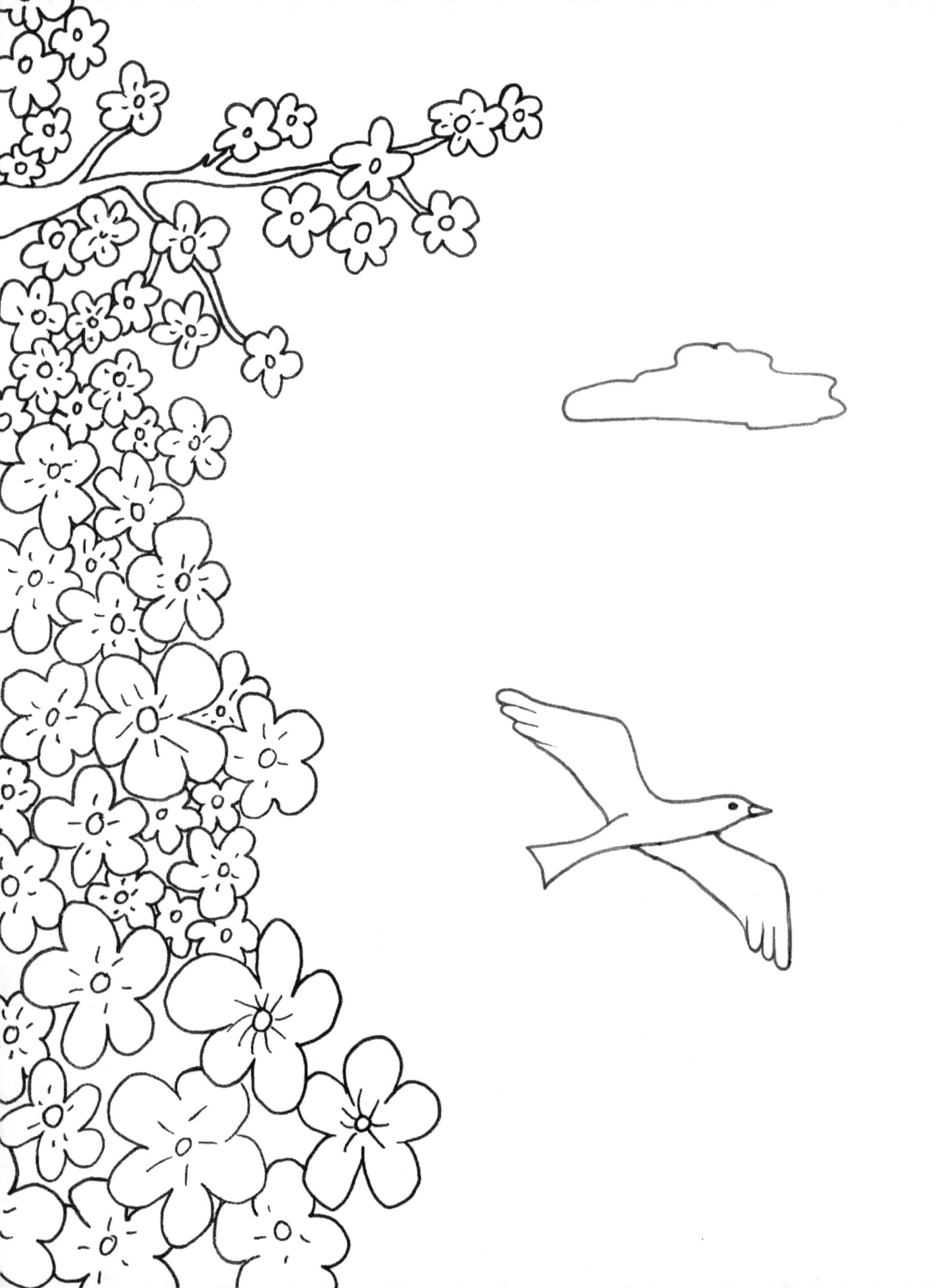

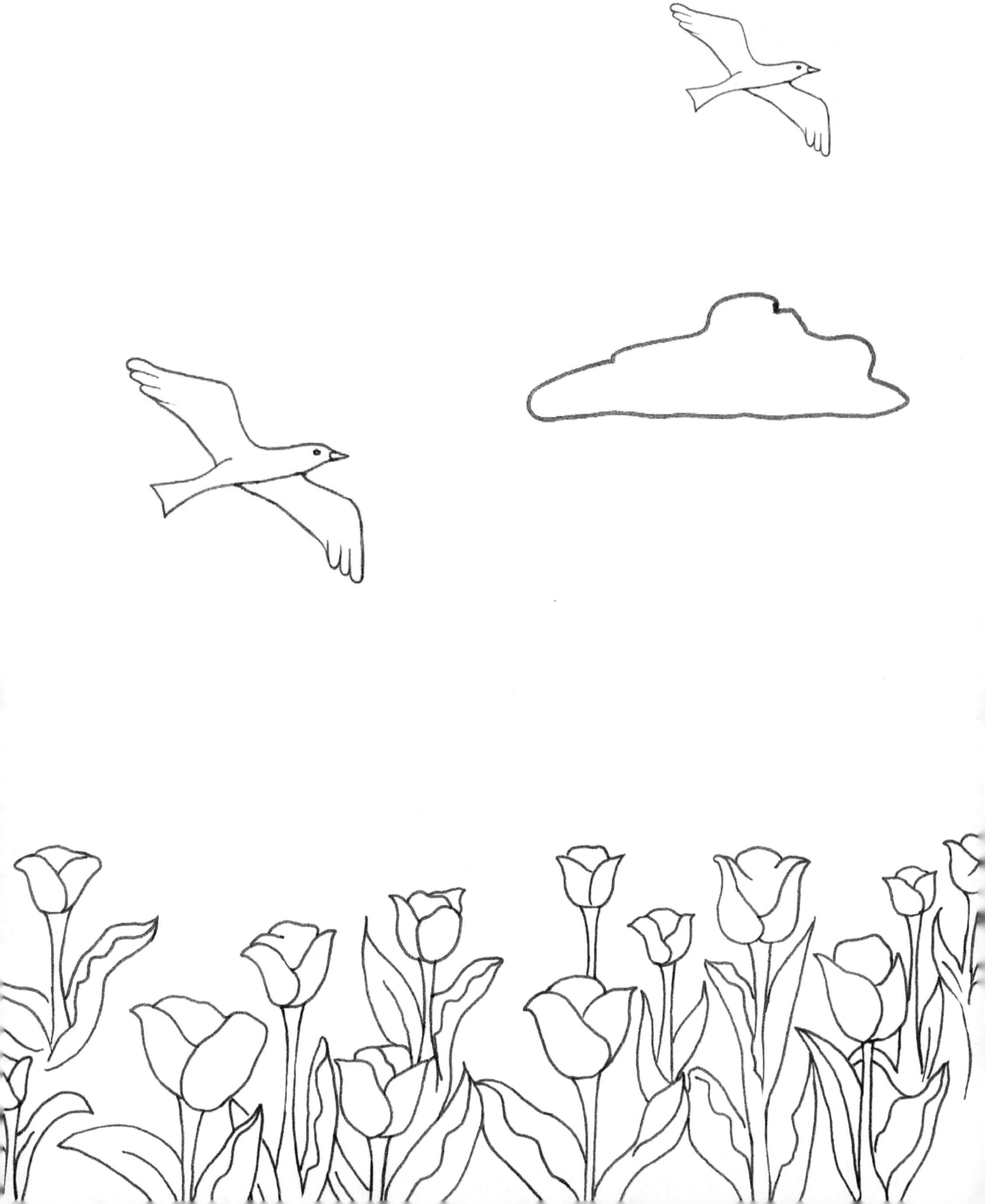

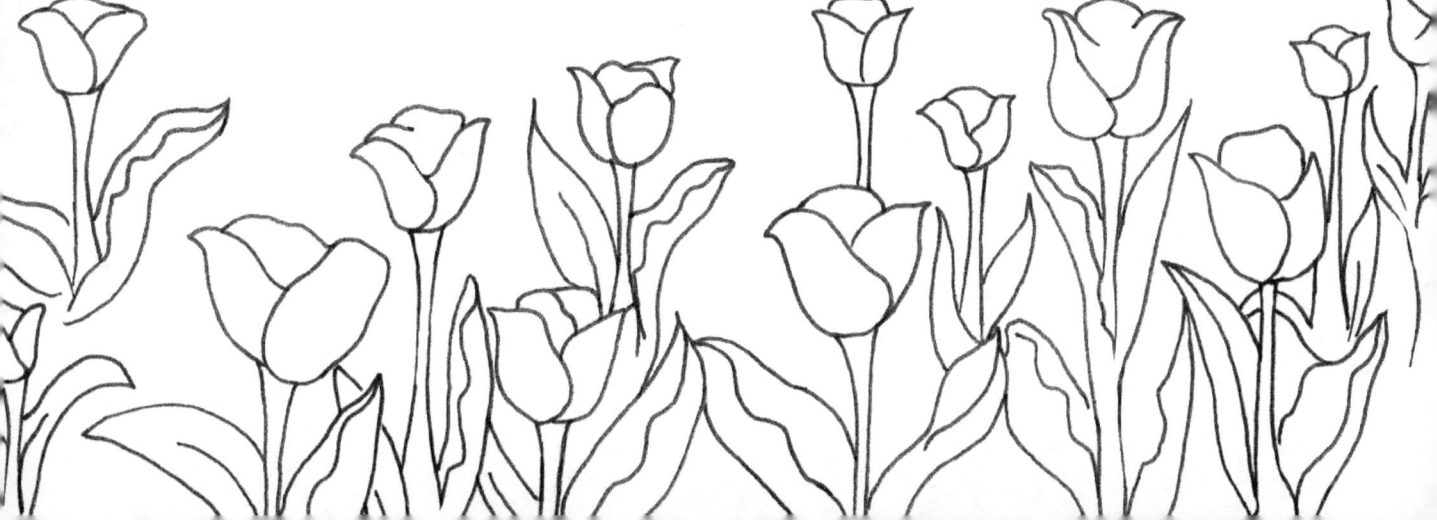

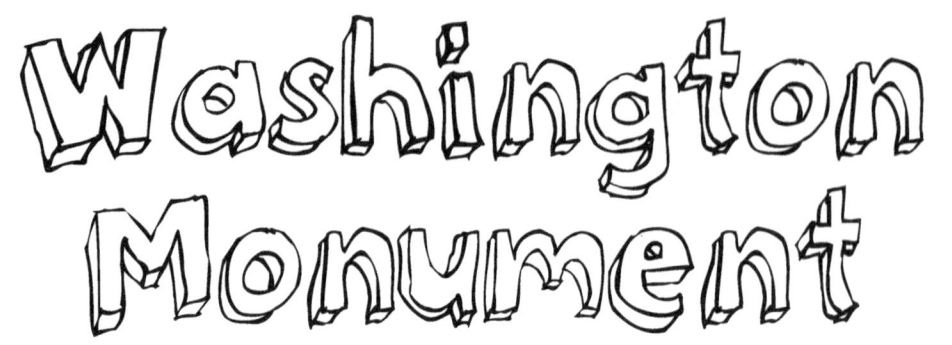

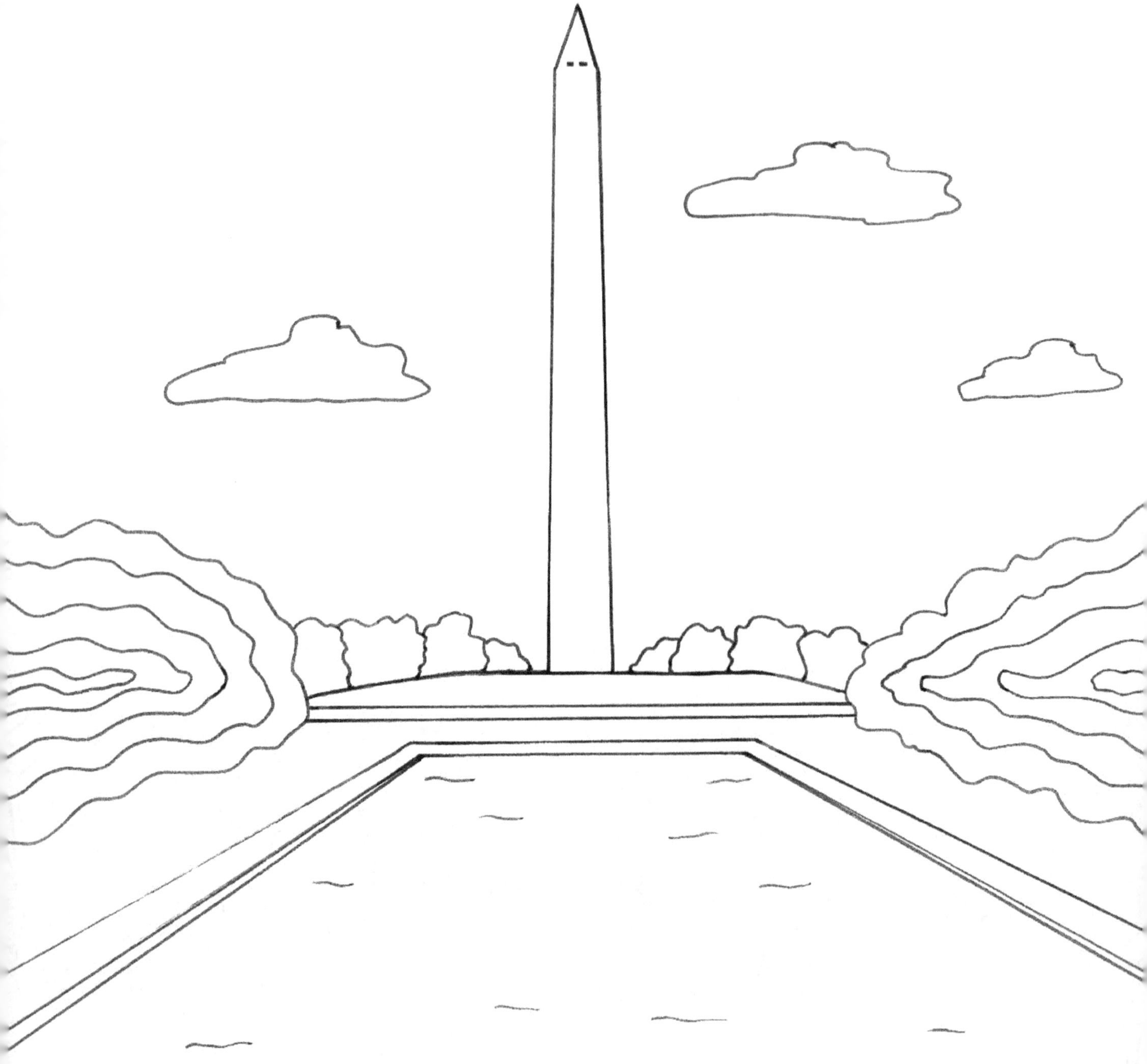

Fun Facts

☆ The Washington Monument is **555 ft.** and 5 1/8in. high.

☆ It has **50** flights of stairs.

☆ It weighs more than **81,000** tons.

☆ It opened to the pubic on October 9, **1888.**

☆ This monument to George Washington, America's first President, was begun in his lifetime, but it wasn't finished until a century later when Chester A. Arthur, the 21st President, was in office.

☆ George **Washington** himself stopped plans for the monument due to lack of government funds. He didn't want to use public money for the project.

☆ In **1833** the Washington National Monument Society was founded to raise private funds for the project.

☆ On July 4, **1848** the cornerstone was laid. It contained a box of items such as a portrait of George Washington, newspapers, U.S. coins and a copy of the Constitution.

☆ In **1854** funds ran low again and work came to a standstill. The monument was **150 ft.** high. Construction remained on hold through the Civil War.

☆ In **1876,** spurred by the **100th anniversary** of America's founding, President Ulysses Grant authorized federal funding to finish the project.

☆ The original stone used for the first 150 ft. could not be matched when construction began again. You can see the different shades of the two stones from each construction period.

Historical Rowhouses

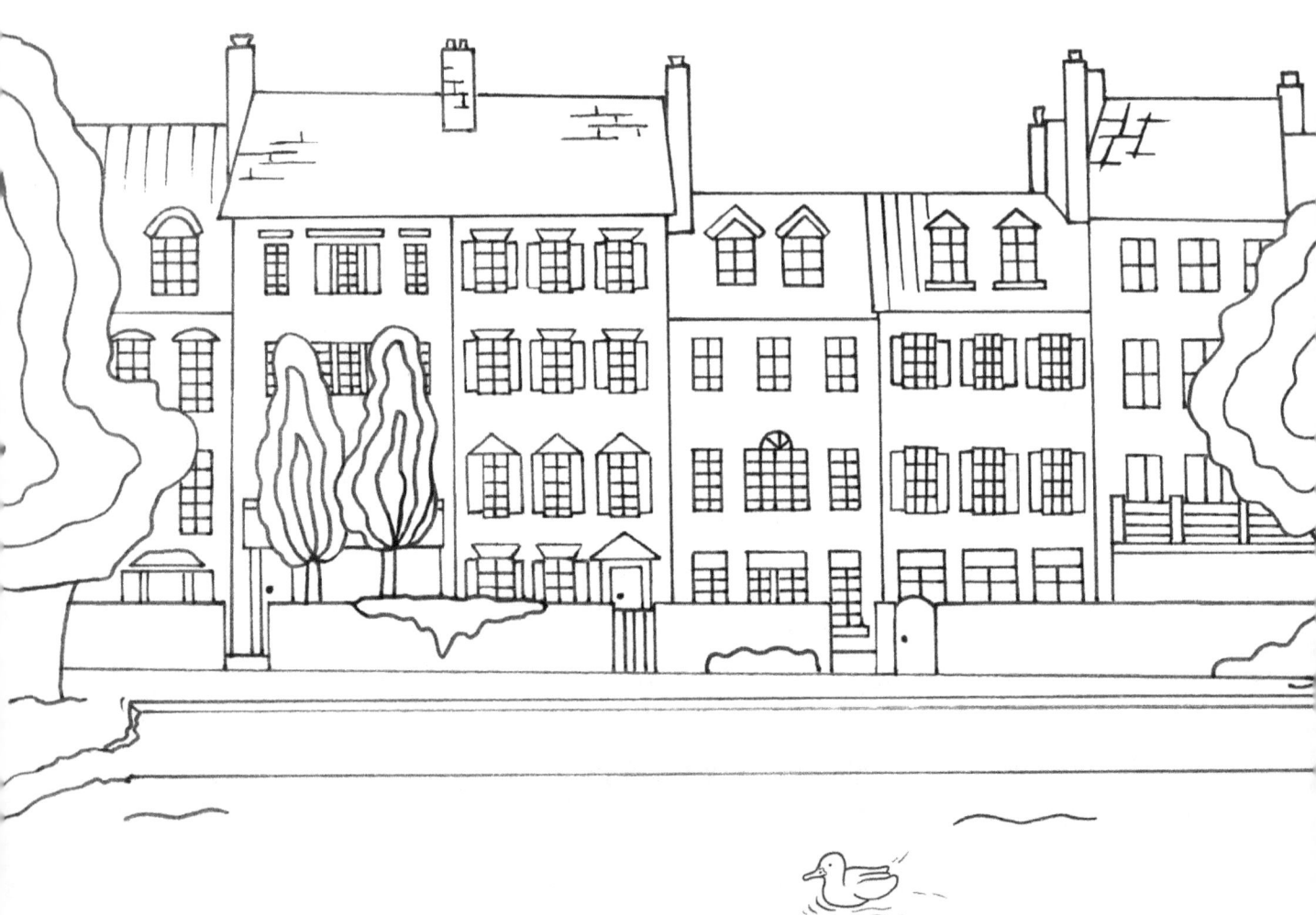

☆ Washington D.C. was established in **1790** when an act of Congress authorized a federal district along the Potomac River.

☆ Washington D.C. was designed by Pierre Charles **L'Enfant**.

☆ Washington's nearly **250 year** history of domestic architecture shows a range of periods, styles, and types. It is remarkable for the nearly intact survival of many eighteenth and nineteenth-century residential neighborhoods.

☆ Until single-family houses were built beginning in the 1850s, **rowhouses** were the major house style in Washington.

☆ Long, rectangular lots were designed specifically to promote the rowhouses style.

☆ The city's building regulations stipulated that **brick and stone** be used. Houses could be no more than **40 ft.** tall. Houses built on the avenues had to be at least 35 ft. tall.

☆ All buildings were to be parallel to the streets.

☆ Many of the mid-to-late nineteenth and twentieth-century suburban neighborhoods (within the city's boundaries as well as many in Maryland and Virginia) have been maintained in their **original style**.

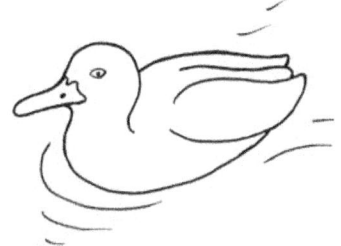

Key Bridge

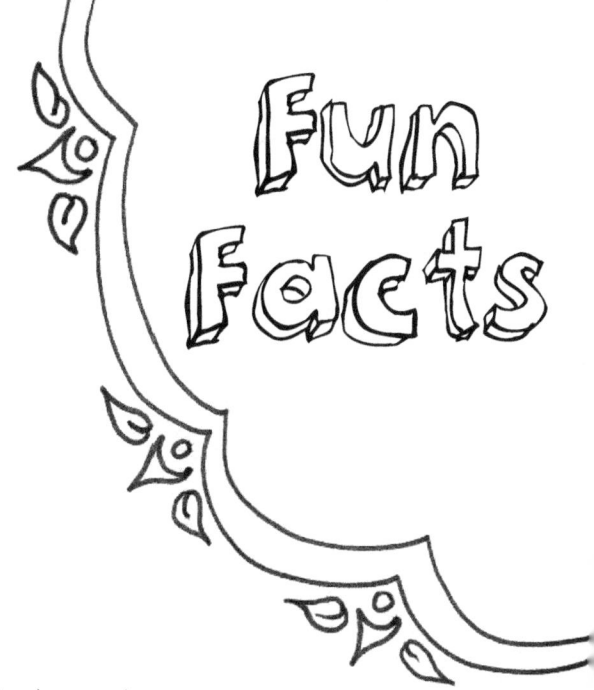

Fun Facts

☆ The Key Bridge was built in **1923**.

☆ It is **518m** long.

☆ It was named after **Francis Scott Key** who wrote the Star Spangled Banner, and whose home was just a few blocks from the bridge.

☆ It was designed by Nathan C. **Wyeth** and Max C. **Tyler**.

☆ The Key Bridge spans the **Potomac** River, connecting Washington D.C.'s Georgetown neighborhood with Arlington County, Virginia's Rosslyn neighborhood.

☆ The Key Bridge replaced an old aqueduct bridge. The first aqueduct bridge was built in **1830** to carry the Chesapeake and Ohio Canal across the Potomac.

☆ The bridge was converted into a roadway during the Civil War.

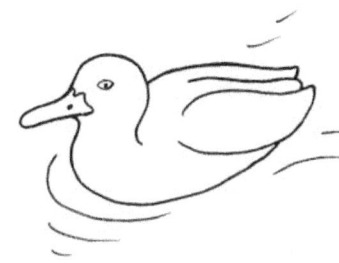

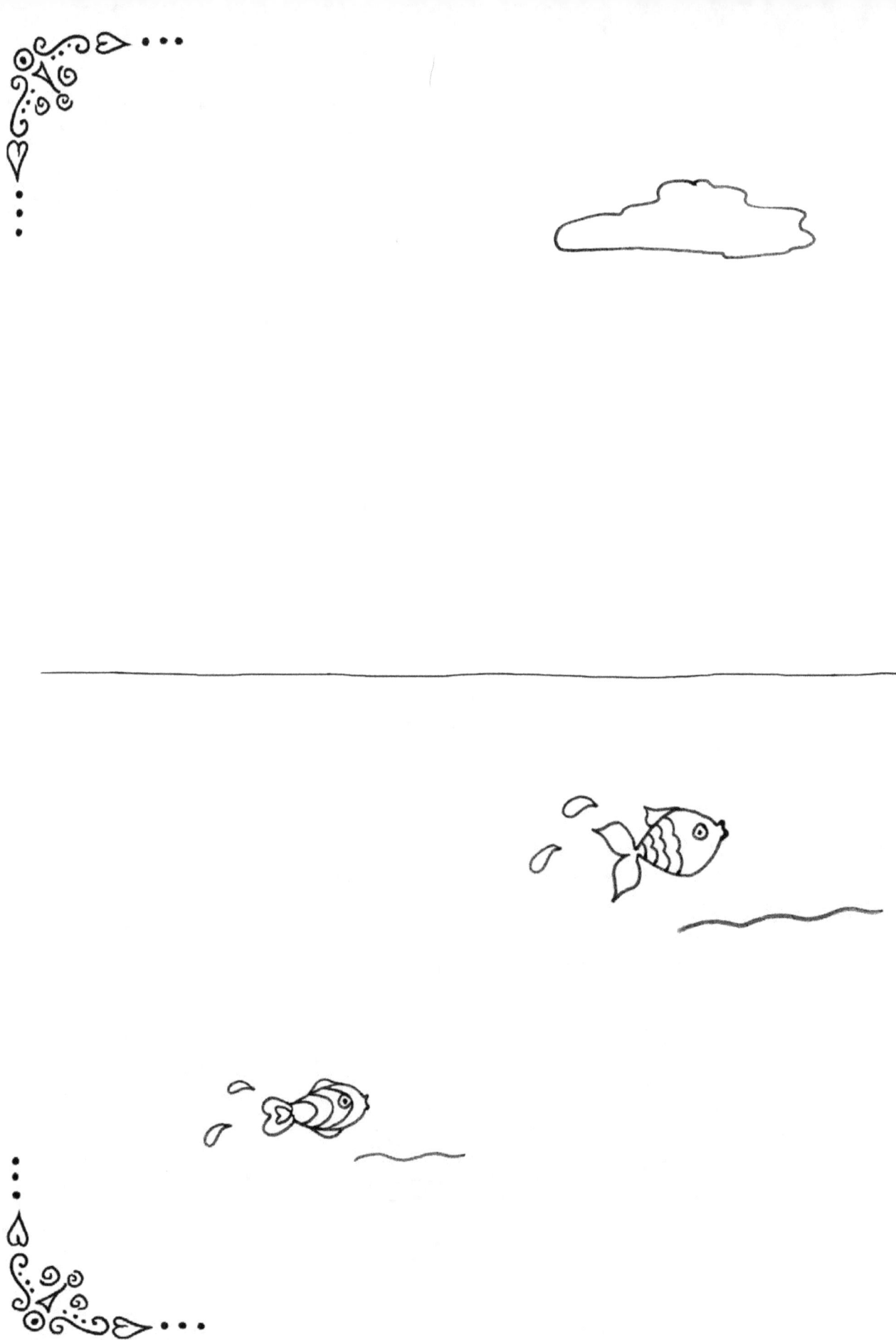

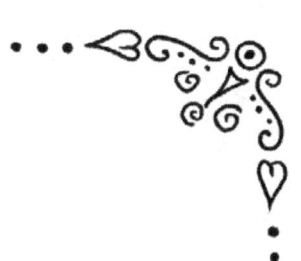

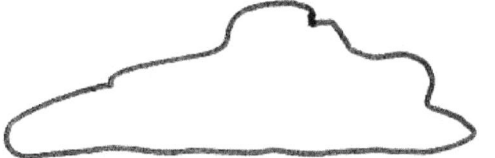

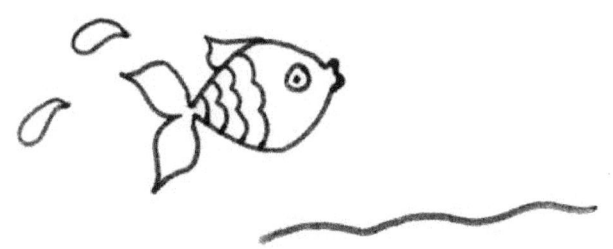

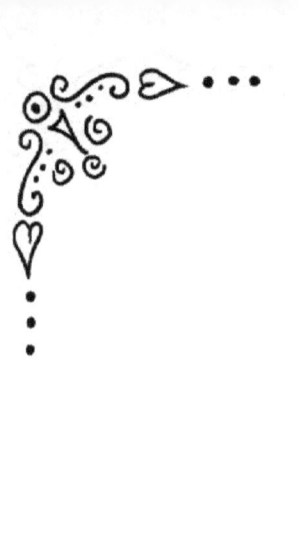

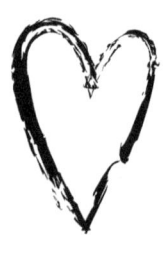

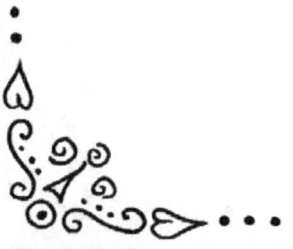